Twats

Celebrities, wannabes
and nobodies

by
Marc Blake

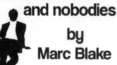

Crombie Jardine
PUBLISHING LIMITED
www.crombiejardine.com

This edition was first published by
Crombie Jardine Publishing Limited in 2006

ISBN 1-905102-34-8

Written by Marc Blake
Cover design by Stewart Ferris

Printed and bound in the United Kingdom by
William Clowes Ltd, Beccles, Suffolk

CONTENTS

FOREWORD

There are twats everywhere: your boss, the guy you work with, your in-laws, your friends – even *you* might be a twat. But the *real* twats are those people on TV who won't get out of your face:

Celebrity twats

Former politicians. Spit-roasting footballers, reality TV show contestants. Boy bands, vacuous actors, 'it' girls, skeletal Supermodels... It's the barrel-scraping twats of 'D' list fame; the disgraced, the dumb and the dumbed down who need namin' and shamin' for being complete and utter

PRATS
&
TWATS!

INDUSTRIES CONTAINING A MINIMUM OF 80% TWATS

Rap/Rock

Film

Meeja

Fashion

Politics

 Sport

IT

WHY SUPERMODELS ARE TWATS...

Being 6 feet and as thin as a twiglet does not constitute a superpower.

Read their lips on the catwalk. 'Left, right, left...'

Cocaine is not a food group.

**Smiling and pouting is
not a hard day's work.**

**Rehab is not a
Muslim garment.**

**The answer to the
question 'Why are we
here?' is not 'For the free
shoes and drugs.'**

**Air kissing is not a
real greeting unless
you are French.**

WHY FOOTBALLERS ARE TWATS...

You cannot give
110% to anything.

At the end of the
day it gets dark.

Of course it's a
game of two halves.

**Conceding a goal
is still losing 1-nil.**

**Putting on the pressure
is still fouling.**

**Match fit does not mean
a spit roast in your hotel
the night before.**

Roy Keane.

WHY ACTORS
ARE PRATS...

**It's not rocket science,
it's pretending.**

**Most of your job involves
hanging around for vast
sums of money.**

**You are nothing without
a decent script.**

 12

**Getting into 'character'
means funny accent,
funny wig.**

**Everybody is not
'super to work with'.
They are tolerating you
because they have to.**

You are all dispensable.

WHY POLITICIANS ARE TWATS...

Spending more time with your family means your 'new' family.

'I've always maintained this position' refers to one of wheedling and lying.

14

**The 'facts' of the matter
are spurious statistics.**

**The 'honourable member'
ought to be kept in
your pants.**

**'Tough choices' never
affect you, you rich twat.**

**Everything you say
and do is a denial or a
smokescreen.**

WHY TV PUNDITS ARE TWATS...

You are an expert in
WHAT exactly?

We are not watching
for your 'hilarious'
anecdotes.

**Everyone has an opinion.
All you have is a
better agent.**

**If you need a caption
for your profession
– you don't have one.**

**100 Best Telly Nose-
Picking moments has not
'captured the mood
of the nation'.**

HOW TO SPOT TWATS WHO HAVE HAD 'WORK' DONE

They claim it's a new diet.

They get a new boyfriend/ husband to go with the new breasts.

Faint marker-pen lines.

**Eyebrows fixed
in a permanent rictus
of shock.**

**They have no facial
expression whatsoever.**

**They recoil from
an air-kiss.**

No earlobes.

**Nostrils too small to
ingest powder.**

'PROFESSIONALS' WHO WORK WITH TWATS

Nail technicians

Beauty therapists

Stylists
(house, garden, hair, dog)

**Psychics
and/or healers**

Yoga instructors

**Celebrity doctors/
gynaecologists**

**Gym instructors/
sex partners**

Stalkers

HELLO! SYNONYMS FOR RUTTING LIKE FERAL DOGS ON HEAT

'Spotted together'

'Whirlwind romance'

'Romantically linked'

**'Getting to know
each other'**

'Getting cosy'

**'Are taking
things slowly
at the moment'**

HOW MUCH OF A CELEBRITY TWAT IS SHE?

Measures her fame in column inches.

Complains about stalkers, because she doesn't have one.

**Forgets who her
on/off relationship
is supposed to be
with this week.**

Has blonde moments.

**Says 'It's just great
to be nominated'.**

Says 'You like me...
you really like me'
(what a Gwyneth!).

Has a designer baby
as an accessory.

Claims to have given
birth without painkillers.

**And then shrinks
back to a size
eight within a week.**

**Stages regular
comebacks with ever
more outrageous
costumes.**

HOW MUCH OF A CELEBRITY PRAT IS HE?

Sports obscure Celtic, Aramaic or badly spelt tattoos.

Has an entourage that contains big black guys solely for street cool.

Insists on being called by one name (yes you Bonio!)

Informs the papers when he's going jogging.

Has any kind of haircut that resembles a fin.

Claims to be 'actually quite shy'.

Denies bisexuality when Popbitch and Holy Moly have been exposing it for months.

Likes to 'party' i.e. enjoys cocaine.

30

TWAT NAMES

Clarissa

 Trinny

Tara

Gordon

Jordan

Paris

Darius

Sudoku

CELEBRITY NAMES STILL AVAILABLE FOR PRAT BABIES

Spatula

Heimlich

Fungus

Ratatouille

Streatham

Heston

 Spavin

Orange Pippin

Orinoco

Weetabix

RUBBISH DVD 'EXTRAS'

Director's commentary

The same film but with an autistic fan-boy gibbering in the background.

Deleted scenes

There's a reason why they did not make the final cut. They're shite.

Director's cut

The beardy man's version – twice as long and twice as dull as the studio-released flick.

Easter eggs

Oh, big surprise for all that effort in finding them.

Cast biogs

A list of the other embarrassingly crap films the stars appeared in.

Language selection

My sole reason for buying this DVD was to learn Mandarin or Flemish.

Storyboard

The cartoon version of the story.

Costumes

Unless it's women in skin tight latex, what's the point?

Animated menu

In a restaurant I don't expect the waiter to *dance* the sodding menu for me, do I?

'Making of' documentary

You will watch this once. It will destroy your subsequent enjoyment of the film.

Blooper reel

Actors fucking about and fucking up. Fuck off.

WHEN TWATS MARRY

*… thankfully making
two people miserable
instead of four*

David and Victoria

Jordan and Peter

Jude and Sienna

Cameron and Justin

Richard and Judy

Courtney Love and anyone

CELEBRITY MARRIAGES THAT LASTED A YEAR

**Carrie Fisher to
Paul Simon in 1983**

**Courtney Love to
James Moreland in 1989**

**Drew Barrymore to
Jeremy Thomas in 1994**

Elizabeth Taylor to Conrad Hilton Jr. 1950

Eminem to Kim Mathers in 1999

Geena Davis to Richard Emmolo in 1982

Janet Jackson to James DeBarge in 1984

**Jennifer Lopez to
Ojani Noa in 1997**

**Robin Givens to
Mike Tyson in 1988**

**Shannen Doherty to
Ashley Hamilton in 1993**

CELEBRITY MARRIAGES THAT LASTED TWO DAYS

Britney Spears married Jason Allen Alexander in 2004.

The marriage was annulled a whole two days later.

SIGNS THAT YOUR TWATTING POP CAREER IS OVER

You 'concentrate on other projects'.

You change your record company.

 44

**Your last single
topped the charts...
in the Ukraine.**

**You slag off X Factor for
the column inches.**

**You have
'creative differences'
with your producer.**

**You say
'I still have a record deal'.**

SIGNS THAT THE CELEBRITY RELATIONSHIP IS OVER

A denial is issued by the PR Company.

Tabloid gossip begins 'according to tabloid gossip'.

You make public appearances together.

Rumours about the state of the marriage come from 'friends', 'insiders' and 'a source'.

You are spotted leaving the tattoo-removal parlour.

You are seen with a 'mystery blonde'.

You appear on red carpets...thousands of miles apart.

You are 'consoled by a close friend'.

The 'close friend' is of the same sex.

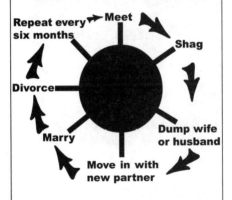

CELEBRITY RELATIONSHIP CURVE

Repeat every six months → Meet

Shag

Dump wife or husband

Move in with new partner

Marry

Divorce

49

LIES ABOUT MOVIES AND WHAT THEY MEAN

A great script.
We've fired the writer.

A dream to work with.
He locked himself in his trailer.

I really felt for the character.
Tears of joy at getting £14m.

Based on a true story.
We put an American
in to get funding.

The motion picture event of the year.
Not this year.

FILM STAR INTERVIEW QUESTIONS AND WHAT THEY MEAN

 ## What's the new movie about?

Same old shit or are you wearing a wig this time?

Did you identify with the character?

Let's see how vain
you really are...

Do you watch your old movies?

You've made some
right turkeys in the past.

This role seems an odd choice for you?

Couldn't you get
the lead role?

Was it hard preparing for the role?

How was the trailer?

You've worked with this director twice now...

Will no one else hire you?

What's the movie you're most proud of?

You used to make good films. Remind me…?

What was it like working with your co-star?

What was it like sleeping with your co-star?

How do you feel when you read the press?

That salacious rumour is not going away.

What's next in the pipeline?

Got any more work or are you off to the theatre?

BIZARRE TWAT RELIGIONS

Anything with Shakras

Raiki

Scientology

Sufi

Sudoku

Buddhism

Bulimia

CELEBRITY PRAT CLOTHES

'That dress.'
What dress? It's mostly made from boob.

Monkey fur coat.
It looked better on the monkey, actually.

Sunglasses.
Indoors? Do all celebrities have over-sensitive retinas?

CELEBRITY PRAT MANNERISMS

Punching the first photographer they see when arriving at Heathrow.

Covering their face with a towel when putting out the rubbish each morning.

Getting angry when not spotted at the airport or when putting out rubbish.

THANKS FROM THE PODIUM AND WHAT IT REALLY MEANS

This is not for me.
This is so for ME.

So many people to thank.
Those who can further my career.

The Academy.
Or they will never
consider me again.

The film makers.
I never spoke to any of them.

My beautiful co-star.
We shagged, fought,
denied it all.

My director.
Who made Hitler
seem like a fun guy.

My wife.
Who put up with my
absence/whoring
for THREE months.

The producer.
Who has my ass in a vice.

My fellow nominees.
Losers…losers…LOSERS!!!

The writer.
Yeah, right.

CELEB ADJECTIVES EXPLAINED

Thin
Troubled

Love bird
Love child

Over the moon
Out of control

Glowing
Tired

In love
In rehab

Svelte
Skeletal

Brave
Frail

Newly wed
Quickie divorce

Trophy wife
Estranged wife

Gorgeous
Grief-stricken

KEEPING IT REAL: RAP

You are no longer a rap artist when...

Your Homies drive stretch Golf carts.

You have been shot more than once.

You advertise bling for Asprey's.

You duet with a white guy.

Your last album failed to get a parental advisory sticker.

You are seen in a drive-thru not a drive-by.

You get more for your teeth on eBay than for your car.

You fail to get into this years' Ho's Ho.

You are Eminem.

You drop the sugar and the puff and the daddy and now you're just daddy passing the sugar puffs.

CELEBRITY WISDOM

**'Mystery blonde'
sounds better than
'adulterous bitch'.**

**Botox will freeze your
expression for years.
Try not to have it done
at the moment they
hand you the bill.**

**Celebs fear anonymity,
prison and carbohydrates.**

**Acceptance speeches
should be like children.
Short and hysterical.**

**An 'exclusive' is what you
give to journalists...every
15 mins, 25 times a day.**

**Real love is closer than
you think, sometimes
as close as a mirror.**

**Celeb nightmare:
economy class.**

**'Celebrity' is the gap between
wannabe and has-been.**

DO IT YOURSELF CELEBRITY TWAT ARTICLE...

Brave ....

weight battle..........

we can reveal..........

shocked America........

a personal goal........

life changes............

private shame..........

68

friends are asking......

career has taken a back

seat.................

nervous exhaustion......

a source says..........

left alone to live her

life.................

amazing new look!

CELEBRITY LISTS

A List
Parties are thrown in your honour.

B List
You blag your way into A list parties.

C List
You blag your way into B List parties.

D List
You say you were at the A list party.

Z List
You are Peter André.

CELEBRITY PRAT RIGHTS AND WRONGS

Right ☑	Wrong ☒
Asprey's	Argos
Prada	Primark
Bloomingdales	Budgens
New York	Newcastle
Tiara	Tracksuit
Versace	Velour
Jimmy Choo	Clarks
Coke	Crack
Krug	Kronenburg
Cristal	Babycham

CELEBRITY MAXIMS

*If at first you
don't succeed –
pray for a sequel.*

*If there's no biz like
showbiz how come 90% of
actors are not working?*

*Don't ever tick the box
marked no publicity.*

*Don't let money become
your only motivation.
Don't forget revenge…*

*Get away from the glare of
publicity. Host a show on
Channel 5.*

Work your way up from the bottom: this does not necessarily mean anal.

Don't put all your eggs in one basket or if you do, don't give the basket to your agent.

TEN SIGNS THAT YOUR DIET IS OUT OF CONTROL...

Naomi Campbell and Kate Moss are sending you food parcels.

You have to run around in the shower to get wet.

You have a VPL – visible pelvis line.

**You shop in the
children's section.**

**Old Nazis look
at you wistfully.**

**You haven't the strength
to hold the cigarette/
rolled up tenner.**

**You are terrified of
pancakes, bread or chips.**

**Your idea of binge eating
is a crouton and a raisin.**

You fear drains.

**The Sunday Times
asks to photograph you
with flies in your eyes.**

SOUND BITES THAT WE WILL NEVER HEAR

'That's waaaay too much money for so little work...'

'I know – it's brilliant! It's a role in a made-for-TV movie...'

'I have nothing in the pipeline.'

'He was a cunting
cunt to work with.'

'Charity?
Bollocks to that!'

'Let's not use
lawyers...'

 80

'The rumours are all true. I fuck trees. Ooh you dirty little sapling.'

'That sick child is not ugly enough for me to appear with.'

CELEBRITY MAXIMS 2: THE REVENGE

*An apple a day
is more than a model
eats in a week.*

82

*Fame is a fickle
mistress… which
makes Abi Titmuss
very famous indeed.*

*Good PR will
sort out the fact
from the fiction...
and print the fiction.*

Have a famous husband….
preferably someone else's.

In the future everyone
will be famous...
for being famous for
fifteen minutes.

84

When you kiss and tell,
first stow away heavy
objects, like lawyers.

"SPECIAL THANKS TO..." TWAT STUFF THEY WRITE ON THE CD

Mum and Dad.
(For keeping out of the papers.)

The greats.
(i.e. the black blues players
whose ideas I ripped off.)

**My chiropractor/
homeopath/
acupuncturist.**
(I am in PAIN.)

God and Jack Daniels.
(Not in that order.)

**Fender, Les Paul and
Gibson Guitars.
Zildjian cymbals.
Marshall amps.**
(Because they give
them to me free.)

The Record Company.
(Please give me
another deal.)

**The Studio,
for 'sonic brilliance'.**
(Drugs and patience.)

**Obscure people with
nicknames. Crocodile.
Rita the footeater.
Tremendous Brian.**
(They have the cellphone images.)

The manager.
(Or I might find myself in the trunk of a car…)

All our fans who put us where we are.
(Please stop downloading.)

The road crew.
(For procuring the finest hookers, jailbait and chemicals.)

HOW TO ACT LIKE A CELEBRITY TWAT

In a lift you preen in the mirror and ask '...Penthouse?'

You sign for a parcel asking '...and who shall I make it out to?'

You wear shades in bed.

**You pat your pregnant
wife's stomach as proof of
your fertility.**

**You make your home look
like an art gallery,
surrounded by guards and
full of expensive rubbish.**

**You make an impromptu
acceptance speech
to the postman.**

**You throw a wobbly in a fish
and chip shop because you
'cannot tolerate carbs'.**

THE BIGGEST CELEBRITY LIE

'I can't find a partner.'

AND 7 MORE FOR GOOD MEASURE

'I had never watched the show
before I was invited on.'

'I like to spend time
with my family.'

'We're really happy.'

'I have no comment.'

'I hate the paparazzi.'

'What do I like in a man?
Humour and sensitivity.'

'I'm not graceful...
I'm really clumsy.'

THE A-Z OF CELEBRITY TWATTAGE

Accessories
Belt, shoes, baby.

Bulimia
The only way her colon will see meat is if she does anal.

Cell phone
Direct line to publicist, AA and anorexia helpline.

Drug habit
Eyeballs dilated. Nostrils flaring, septum missing.

Entourage
PR, A&R, leeches, other scum and agents.

Flying
Never seen anywhere other than Club Class.

Gucci
First word said to celeb baby.

Hangers-on
Family members who have the negatives. ★

Jetlag
Coke lag.

★

Ketamine
Horse tranquiliser. Use in case of emergency – if sleeping with Darius, Chico or Jade.

Luggage
Minimal. The drugs are in the nanny's stomach.

★

Makeup

Too much. Trowel for Mrs Beckham, please...

Names

The more names the lower the I.Q.

E.g. Tara-Pratter-Tomkinson
Hugh Fernley–Prattingstall
Laurence Llewelyn-Praten

Operation scars

Too posh to push.
Your stomach looks like a letterbox.

Publicist
Always to hand if you need a comment from a 'close friend'. ★

Queue
Never ever queue.

Red carpet
There's even one in front of your cat door. ★

Shiatsu
A dog? A massage? As long as it sounds oriental it's cool.

★

Tattoo

Men – Celtic blarney.
Women – arse, ankle or
shoulder. Compulsory.

Ugly

God gave us plastic surgery.
There is no excuse.

Versace

Famous fashion designer.
Shoots you, sir.

Walk

Always teeter. Flat shoes
are for civilians and lesbians.

Xxx
What you did before X Factor.

Y Factor
What we think of X Factor contestants.

Zip
Zip and tuck...could be the next fashionable op?

CELEBRITY BABIES...

**Nappies by
Stella McCartney.**

4 by 4 buggies.

**Christening present
is a coke spoon.**

**Their first words:
'Mummy's in rehab'.**

**Parenting by nannies,
then step-parents
then therapist.**

YOU HAVE HAD TOO MUCH WORK DONE WHEN...

Michael Jackson starts to look normal.

You cannot go near a radiator.

**You cannot
swim underwater
because you contain
too much saline.**

**Joan Rivers starts
making jokes
about you.**

**Every time you smile
your ears pop.**

Your testicles look like marbles.

Anal bleaching isn't going far enough.

You use words like 'inner beauty' and 'peace'.

WHAT PRATS SAY...
WHAT PRATS MEAN...

A man's man
Gay

A girly girl
Likes shopping

Broke down
Phoned his/her publicist

Friends rallied round
**Publicists worked all
night to spin story**

My friends are my family
I disowned my real family

Girl next door glamour
Ugly

Trademark style
Jeans and a bare midriff

A brave face
A coked-up face

Picking up the pieces
Up for meaningless sex

Thrown herself into her work
Grabs all she can before celebrity expires

DECODING RECORD COMPANY PUBLICITY PRATTAGE

The defining record of the decade
The defining record of the week

Word of mouth sensation
We pay students to say nice things

Committed to touring
Committed to working off the huge
advance

Eclectic style
Tuneless

**Breaking the
rules of rock**
Tuneless nonsense

Has a dance element
Fearless bandwagon jumpers

GOOD THINGS REALITY TV HAS DONE...

Taught Chavs to use a bandsaw...

Matched verbally abusive husbands with obnoxious bitches.

**Proved that we
really can't be
arsed to cook.**

**Directed
dysfunctional people
toward a full mental
breakdown.**

**Lowered the price of
unsaleable homes by
painting walls the
colour of vomit.**

NOTES FOR TV PRESENTER TWATS!

Stop telling us what's coming up and provide some actual content!

It's not stone, barley or pale ochre – its fucking beige!

Stop *emphasizing* all the *wrong* words.

Don't pretend that £500 of MDF and a few tassels is a makeover when it's a stage set.

Stop telling people how they ought to feel.

Stop trying to make a silk babe out of a sow.

REALITY SHOWS WE'D ACTUALLY LIKE TO SEE

Death Row Cuisine

★

Changing Organs

★

Cannibal Cook-Out

★

Knife Swap

★

I've Been Shot!

I'm a Former Celebrity – Leave Me in the Jungle

★

Fuck me? Fuck you!

★

Big Baghdad Brother

★

Plop Idol

★

Pond Swap

★

Xxx Factor

IF ALL ELSE FAILS...

Stop being a prat and get a real job!

AFTERWORD

Marc Blake is neither a prat nor a twat. A comedian and comedy writer, he once ticked the box marked 'no publicity' and has been suffering for it ever since.

He has had the privilege of working with celebrity prats, twats and even agents and has found them without exception to be the wittiest and most attractive people in their own minds.

He can be seen in the pages of 'Owoite' Magazine (south London's *Hello*) or found on his website www.marcblake.net, where he lives.

ISBN 1-905102-21-6, £2.99

Shag

yourself slim

The most enjoyable way to lose weight

Imah Goer

ISBN 1-905102-03-8, £2.99

ISBN 1-905102-17-8, £2.99

The Little Book of Chavs

The Branded Guide to Britain's New Elite

LEE BOK

UPDATED

ISBN 1-905102-01-1, £2.99